Sand Lake town
Library

WILD WORDS!

How to Train Them to Tell Stories

WILD WORDS!

How to Train Them to Tell Stories

by Sandy Asher

Illustrated by Dennis Kendrick

Walker and Company
New York

First published in the United States of America in 1989
by Walker Publishing Company, Inc.

Published simultaneously in Canada by Thomas Allen & Son
Canada, Limited, Markham, Ontario.

Library of Congress Cataloging-in-Publication Data

Asher, Sandy.
Wild words! How to train them to tell stories/by Sandy Asher;
illustrated by Dennis Kendrick.
p.   cm.
Bibliography: p.
Includes index.
Summary: Presents advice for budding writers on how to put ideas down on paper
in language that is expressive and literate, how to bring characters to life, how to
line up a plot, and how to polish the final product.
1. Language arts (Elementary)—Juvenile literature.   2. Creative
writing—Juvenile literature.   [1. Creative writing.]
I. Kendrick, Dennis, ill.   II. Title.
LB 1576.A715   1989   89-5692
372.6—dc20   CIP
AC
ISBN 0-8027-6887-3.   ISBN 0-8027-6888-1 (lib. bdg.).
Printed in the United States of America

1   3   5   7   9   10   8   6   4   2

Book design by Laurie McBarnette

To Serina, Ann, Kate, Tanya, Stacey, Ichiro, Andy, Melissa, Bryan, Rachel, Beth, Tammison, Rhonda, and Patrick, and to the teachers who have encouraged and inspired them.

With special thanks to Joyce Pyle, fifth grade teacher, Bingham School; John H. Bushman, Director, The Writing Conference; The Institute of Children's Literature; The National Association for Young Writers; and Venita Bridger, Language Arts Supervisor, Springfield, MO, Public Schools.

ACKNOWLEDGMENTS:

Material in Chapter six appeared in "Show; Don't Tell," by Sandy Asher, Copyright 1988: The Institute of Children's Literature.

Portions of Chapters four and five appeared in "Rocky Balboa vs. Ebenezer Scrooge," by Sandy Asher, *The SCBW Bulletin*, May/June, 1988. Copyright 1988: Society of Children's Book Writers.

The following stories and poems originally appeared in *Unicorns and Daisies*, a publication of Springfield, Missouri, Public Schools:

"A Bath and Some Clothes Are All She Needed," by Stacy Inmon; "The Attic," by Bryan Smith; "The Dragon Friend," by Rachel Violet Grand; "Spiders," by Patrick Colvand.

The following material appeared in *1988 Writing Camp Collections*, a publication of The Writing Conference, Ottawa, Kansas:

"My Party," by Serina Desch; "An Interruption before Spring," by Ann E. Zitterkopf; "The Call," by Kate Moore; "The Adventures of Ter-Ter," by Beth A. Montgomery.

Portions of Chapter nine appeared in "What's In It for You?" by Sandy Asher, in *The Writer's Slate*, a publication of The Writing Conference, Ottawa, Kansas, and in "Paper Panic: One Writer's Crusade," by Sandy Asher, in the *National Association of Young Writers newsletter*.

Contents

1

Wild Words! Proceed With Caution

Have you ever had something happen to you and your friends that was falling-down-on-the-floor funny? And the next day, when you tried to tell someone else all about it, that person listened to your story and never once cracked a smile?

What went wrong? You could see that hilarious scene in your mind as clearly as if it were still happening. You chose perfectly good words to describe it. In fact, the story was so funny, you laughed the whole time you told it. And all you got back from your listener was a puzzled look and "What's so funny about that?"

Words don't always do what we expect them to. Written words can be even trickier than spoken words. When we speak we can use the sound of our voices to show what we mean: loud for anger, soft for soothing. If that isn't enough, we can wave our hands, raise our eyebrows, wiggle our noses, or stamp our feet to get the point across.

But when we write, our faces, voices, and bodies stay home. Only our words go out into the world. Words are not thoughts or feelings or the pictures in our heads. They're part of a code—language. We take the pictures and ideas in our heads and make squiggly marks on paper to represent them. Then other people have to look at those marks and see pictures and ideas again. It's not easy!

When it works, it's wonderful. Stories and poems and plays—even notes passed in class—make us see the world in new ways, through the eyes of the writer.

But sometimes it doesn't work. Words run wild. The code carries the wrong message. What happens then is definitely not wonderful. Funny stories fall flat. Sad stories get giggles. People think we're angry when we're kidding. Or they think we're kidding when we're angry.

When you write a story, what you have to say is important. You don't want it to come across scrambled. This book is about making the code work. It will help you train those wild words to tell your stories the way you want them told.

2

Pin Down Ideas

Grocery list, letter, or story, all writing starts with an idea. Ideas for writing are everywhere. There are more than enough to go around. In fact, in a room full of writers, ONE idea is enough to go around.

One morning, I gave twenty-nine young writers the exact same idea to write about. Twenty-nine heads bent over pads of paper. Twenty-nine pens scritched and scratched in unison.

Did they all write the same thing? Absolutely not. Each and every writer wrote something new and different.

This was the idea: Somewhere, a phone is ringing. Who hears it? Who is calling? What happens next?

Here are a few of the responses to that idea. The first caller is an irate parent.

My Party
by Serina Desch
7th grade

My parents had just left for the weekend. As soon as they pulled out of the driveway, I jumped up and down in excitement. I had invited over a couple of friends to have a small party.

Well, my couple of friends turned out to be about fifteen more than I could handle. It was all right until everybody started acting wild and throwing things around. On top of all that, the television was blaring.

I heard something that sounded like a cricket. It was the telephone. I rushed to answer it, but by the time I got there, I got nothing but a dial tone. Well, I thought, maybe they'll call back.

After a few minutes, a smell wafted through the air. Pizza! First, there were more people than I'd invited, and now they were eating my food!

The phone rang again, and I answered it. I snapped a sarcastic hello. It was my mother. I was busted.

"What is going on?" she asked.

"I'm just having a fun time," I replied.

"Doing what?" she asked.

"Having fun," I said.

"Your fun had better end soon because we're coming home."

"All right," I stuttered. "I'll send everyone home."

The house was trashed. There were cans and food on the floor, plus all the dishes. I finished cleaning up just as my parents walked in. They slammed the door and gave me dirty looks. I knew I was in deep trouble.

The second call brings great news!

An Interruption Before Spring
by Ann E. Zitterkopf
11th grade

I turn over. Again, the ear-splitting chirp of the phone pierces my dense, hovering fog. I groan and slide out of bed, hoping my parents will answer it.

This can't be for me, I think. What sane person is awake enough to call another person when that person could be sleeping? Insensitive idiots. But what if something has happened? An emergency? Grandma? Did Jack break up with Jill again?

The wooden floor is cold under my feet. I take gigantic steps to reach the chair on the far side of the room as soon as possible. Another shrill chirp sounds an alarm of worry. I curl my feet underneath me as I sit down. I shiver and curse basement living. I pull the receiver off in the middle of another ring and raise it to my ear.

"Is this Jessica Hartog?" a chipper male voice says.

13

"Yes," I reply, and relax, knowing that if anything were wrong, the caller would immediately ask for my parents.

"Congratulations. You might win—," the voice continues.

"Do you know what time it is?" I mumble.

"Two A.M.," he returns.

"It's two in the morning!" I gasp. "Why are you calling me at this—just a minute. What were you saying?"

"This is Rockin' Rob Stephenson at 96 KMQ. If you can tell us the phrase of the day, you can win a Sony portable CD player."

I sit there, dumbfounded. "Oh, please," I groan, trying to brainstorm a catchy phrase dealing with the radio station.

"That's right!" he screams. Bells sound in the background.

"You've got to be kidding," I respond.

"Nope! Completely serious. 'You've got to be kidding' was our phrase yesterday, though, you listener you! Hop on by the radio station and pick up your new CD player. Thank you for listening to 96 KMQ." The man hangs up.

I fall out of my chair with a thud. My father stumbles through the doorway and asks, "Who in the world is calling you at this time of night?"

"I just won a CD player."

"That's nice, honey." He turns around and starts to leave. "What?"

"Never mind, Daddy. I'll explain in the morning. Good night."

I slump back across my room. I can see crisp frost on part of the windowpane. In bed, the warmth engulfs me.

"How did they get my phone number?" I wonder. "Jill? She's some friend."

I reach over to the clock radio and press the snooze button. "This is 99.1 KNC," the announcer says. I hear Vivaldi's "Spring" as I fall asleep.

And the third call is tragic.

The Call
by Kate Moore
9th grade

Linda grimaced as the cheerful "brrrrring" of the telephone broke the sober silence of the living room. She glanced at her friend Shelly, who sat gnawing on her bottom lip with worry.

"Do you think it's them?" Linda asked, tension tight in her voice. The phone rang again. "Do you want me to get it?"

"Yes, we must find out if he's alive . . . or not," Shelly stated quietly.

Linda reached over a pile of magazines lying on a mahogany coffee table and stretched for the telephone she had kept close since she'd heard news of the terrible accident. It rang again as she came closer to picking up the receiver.

"No," Shelly said faintly. "I'll get it. He's my brother, after all." She stared at the telephone blankly, cracking her knuckles and clearing her throat.

Linda gave her friend a worried look and allowed the telephone to ring two more times. "Oh, for heaven's sake," she cried, impatiently. She picked up the receiver and spoke into it: "Hello?" Agitation was still evident in her voice, but her face mellowed as she listened. "Yes, I see," she said weakly, and flashed Shelly a quick, yet meaningful glance. "Okay," she answered the unseen party, focusing her attention on the telephone cord she was twirling around her finger, "I'll tell her."

Linda hung up the phone slowly and turned to Shelly. She gave Shelly a weak smile and said, "I'm sorry."

How is it possible that one idea, a ringing phone, could inspire so many scenes and styles of writing? What made the difference? What each writer decided to DO with that idea. Both the idea and the writer's response to it are important.

All writers collect ideas. Smart writers write them down. They know words left unwritten can gallop away, taking the idea with them, never to be recaptured.

Anything that attracts your attention is worth jotting down. It may be small or silly or strange, but if it interests you, that's all that matters. You may not write a story about it today, or tomorrow, or next year, or ever. If and when you DO decide to write about it, you'll be glad you kept it safe and sound.

Some writers keep a daily diary. Others keep a file of ideas and toss in newspaper clippings and magazine articles along with their own notes. Still others keep a journal, but don't write in it every day, just when they have something special to record.

Whatever helps you hold onto your ideas is fine. The important thing is to WRITE THEM DOWN. And be sure to include plenty of details. I found a slip of paper in my idea file once that said "Laura—brown hair." That note must have been important to me once or I wouldn't have bothered to write it down. But now I haven't an inkling of who Laura is or why her brown hair was worth remembering.

Tenth grader Tanya Burmaster has an idea for a play. This is how she noted it in her journal:

Play Idea

Cast:
Candice Woodrin—Very religious. Has an inner conflict with herself, thinking she has to be perfect. She thinks, "It's the end of the world if I make a mistake." Soft, feminine looking, with long auburn hair and green eyes. Sixteen years old.
Diana McJenson—Rebellious. Doesn't go to church. Parties a lot. Sixteen years old. Headed for trouble.
Pastor James Finne—Cheery and friendly. Cares a lot about people. Always trying to help people out. Is married and has three grown kids of his own. Late forties.
Alec Hatrik—Diana's boyfriend. Characteristics similar to Diana's. Seventeen years old.
Teachers, congregation, parents, and friends.

Plot:
Candice and Diana get thrown together for a project. They don't get along and they get into arguments. Finally, they confess their problems to each other. They end up teaching each other two important things: it's necessary to have God in your life and it's okay not to be perfect.

Tanya's not sure when she'll develop that idea into a play. Or maybe it'll end up being a story. But until she gets back to it, she knows she's got enough written down to keep the idea alive.

All I know of Laura is
she has brown hair.
Now I'm left to wonder:
Why did I care?
Well-trained words pin ideas down!

3

Bring Characters to Life

A ragamuffin, numbers that gossip, Mr. Nobody—all these characters and more tumble from the pens of young writers. Some seem to be real people:

A Bath and Some Clothes Are All She Needed
by Stacey Inmon
7th grade

Margot was a frail girl who looked as if she had been lost in the rain for years. She had on dull, brown shoes full of big holes. Her faded jeans were cut off at the knees, and all her scrapes and scars stood out against her pale, white skin.

20

The old, gray T-shirt she was wearing was like rags, ripped and torn in every other spot. It hung loosely below her waistline, stretched, with mud stains on it.

Her face was filthy, with dried dirt crumbling off as she moved her mouth. Her long, blond hair was dry and stringy. Margot was so dirty, I did not think she would ever come clean.

My Grandpa
by Ichiro Stewart
5th grade

Promising me
    horses and
    three wheelers
      with love
    not with truth or money.

Telling me stories about
    the old days
    not knowing
      if they're true.

But I love him
    and he loves me.
    I guess that's all that matters.

Others are only doodles:

Desktop Cleaning
by Andy Sears
5th grade

The penciled figures danced all over my desk:
    Scribbles racing,
    Old men singing,
    Shapes swimming,
    Numbers gossiping.
The figures got too crowded one day.
    They had to vanish
    or recess was lost.
I never saw them again.

This one's invisible!

Me and Mr. Nobody
by Melissa Harmon
5th grade

When no one will play with me,
Mr. Nobody will come
    and we'll both play a game.
I can cheat
    and he won't care.
I can goof up
    and he won't mind.
When I'm home alone
we watch something on TV we're not supposed to.
We pop popcorn
    and don't clean up the mess.
But mostly we
    talk about our secrets.

And these are shadows, up to no good:

The Attic
by Bryan Smith
9th grade

My mother told me to get the old television set out of the attic, so she could sell it at the church's poverty fund drive. I went outside to the garage and stood on the stairs, watching the pull string that opened the attic door sway back and forth in the cold, winter air.

As I reached up to pull down the attic door, I thought I heard a sound like an animal whining. I decided it was just the wind and pulled the cord. The door opened with a loud creak, sending chills down my spine. I pulled down the ladder and stepped onto the first rung.

With each step higher, my pulse sped up. Finally I got to the top of the ladder and poked my head through the attic opening. The darkness overwhelmed me. I reached for the string to turn on the light and pulled on it. The light came on for a moment, flickered, and died.

I stepped down to the workbench below and grabbed a flashlight. I also grabbed an ax, just in case. I turned the flashlight on and went up into the attic.

Instantly, the dry air hit me, making me grip the ax handle tighter. The flashlight beamed in front of me, and I saw something move in the flickering shadows. I raised the ax over my head and hurled it towards the shadows. The flashlight reflected off the shiny edge of the ax blade as it flew end over end through the air. It hit a wooden beam and stuck in it. The animal or whatever it was scampered away into the darkness.

I quickly found the small black-and-white television my mother needed and went back down the ladder. I closed the attic door and put the flashlight back on the workbench. I took the old TV into the house and put it onto the kitchen table for my mother. She told me to plug it in, so I did, but the television didn't work. My mother then told me to take it outside and throw it away.

As I turned to go back inside, after I'd thrown the TV away, I heard a scraping sound and the attic door opened and closed quickly. A small piece of paper fluttered out onto the concrete floor of the garage. It said, "Now we have the ax."

Characters may come from real life or from the writer's imagination. Or they may be a combination of the two.

Branching Out,
　　People Soup,
　　　　Whoppers,
　　　　　and Magic
are four ways you can whip up characters of your own.

Branching Out

A branch is not a whole tree, even though they have a lot in common. In the same way, characters are not real people. Real people don't fit into stories. They're too complicated.

While you're reading this book, you may also be doing a dozen other things—all at once! You could be worrying about the sick dog you left at the vet's this morning. You may be hungry. Maybe you're concerned about a test coming up. Or remembering a movie you just saw. Or maybe you're already thinking of a story you'd like to write. At any rate, you're not doing just one thing. You never are. Even your sleep is filled with many dreams.

Characters have to stick to one story at a time. They have to fit that story exactly, with no parts left over or hanging out the sides. Think of the characters in a mystery story. You have to know enough about each of them to decide who committed the crime. But if the writer tried to tell you everything about all of them, the story would bog down in details. The writer would be guilty of killing your interest!

Take another look at the poem, "My Grandpa." This grandfather probably also drives a car and has a job. Perhaps he grows vegetables, plays the ukelele, or owns a pet mouse. Writing about him as a real person, Ichiro could have filled pages and pages with unrelated facts. (Wild words want to do that sometimes!) We'd know more about Grandpa, but the poem would be a shambles.

To create a character for his poem, Ichiro made Grandpa simpler than he really is. He chose just one part of Grandpa's personality to write about: His grandfather makes things up. And he does it with love, wishing he *could* give horses and three wheelers and wishing the old days were as good as his stories about them.

Instead of trying to squeeze a whole tree into his poem, Ichiro included only one branch. Grandpa, a real person, became a character. You can do the same with people you know, or with yourself. You have an unlimited supply of branches!

Here's how:

A. Begin by writing a description of yourself. Make it as detailed as you can. Try to see yourself from many angles by answering these questions:

  1. What do you look like?
  2. What three things do you like best about your personality?

26

3. What three things do you like least about your personality?

4. If you could change yourself in only one way, what would you change and how?

5. Describe your family and how you feel about each member.

6. Who is your favorite person in the world—living or dead, fictional or real—and why is he or she your favorite?

7. Name someone you wish you'd never met or read about or heard of—living or dead, fictional or real—and tell why he or she is your least favorite human being.

8. List six things you enjoy doing.

9. List six things you don't like to do.

10. What are you most proud of in your life and why?

11. If you could change the world in one way, what would you do differently?

12. Describe yourself as you would like to be ten years from today.

Now you know more about yourself than you could ever include in one story. Each bit of information you've written is a branch, a possible character, with a life of his or her own.

B. Go back to questions two and three. You listed six personality traits. Maybe you chose smart, friendly, and kind as those you like, and jealous, shy, and clumsy as those you don't like. Is that possible? How can you be both friendly and shy.

Real people can be one way on Monday and

another way on Tuesday. You're never one way all of the time and you're never all six ways at once. People change by the minute. Characters are more steady.

Choose one of those six traits you've listed. Now think of a character who is almost ALWAYS that way, whether it's cheerful or nervous or friendly or mean. Give that character a name. Write his or her name at the top of a sheet of paper.

Remember, this isn't you anymore. It's a branch, about to grow into a character. You have one personality trait in common, but everything else can be different: name, family, friends, age, hair color, and so on. This character is about to have an adventure you've never had and probably never will.

C. Here we go. Imagine the scene first, then follow the directions carefully.

The scene is a neighborhood fast-food restaurant. Your brand new character is munching a cheeseburger. In walks—can it be? Yes, it is! It's Derf Deefendorf, famous movie director, and he trots right over to your character's table.

"Hi, there," he says. "I'm Derf Deefendorf, and I love the way you are munching that cheeseburger. I'm looking for new talent for my next film, *Big, Bad Burger*, starring that marvelous man himself, Mac Molars. I'd like you to audition for a part. What do you say?"

What DOES your character say? Write it down, keeping his or her branched-out, special personality trait in

mind. Whatever your character says or does, let that personality show.

Some characters will say no and some will say yes. Some won't be able to make up their minds. But whatever your character says, Derf Deefendorf talks him or her into auditioning for a part that very afternoon.

How does your character feel about that? Write it down.

Your character reports to the studio for the audition. "Sorry, the script hasn't been written yet," says Director Deefendorf. "But don't worry. All I want you to do is chat for a few minutes with that marvelous man himself, Mac Molars. The camera will be rolling, but don't even think about that. Relax. Lights, camera, action!"

The camera is on. Mac flashes his marvelous smile at your character and says, "Hi, there. Tell me about yourself."

Your character's mouth opens. What comes out?

Whatever your character says pleases Director Deefendorf. He gives your character a part in the movie—a tiny part. How does your character feel about that? Remember as you write, this character is *not you*.

Your character reports for his or her first day on the movie set. The set is filled with unusual people: actors, crew members, stars, newcomers, and others who just seem to be hanging around. Does your character make friends? If so, with whom? If not, why not?

The film is finished. At a private showing, your character sees that every bit of his or her performance was cut out, except one split second, when he or she thought the camera was turned off and did something foolish. How does your character feel now? Does he or she say anything? Do anything? If so, what—and to whom? If not, why not?

The movie is released and finally comes to a neighborhood theater. Does your character go to see it? If so, when and with whom? If not, why not?

What you have written is not a story. It has no plot. (We'll talk more about plot in Chapters four and five.) Besides, I've set most of the action for you. But you've created a character with a life not at all like yours. (Unless you've been in a Derf Deefendorf movie!) You took a bit of yourself, one trait, and let it branch out in a new direction.

You can do the same with almost any other part of your life or personality you'd like to write about. Or with a part of any other real person you'd like to make into a character. Take one trait, give it a name, and ask it the twelve questions you asked yourself earlier. Every single answer will be different from yours, because your characters are not you. They're not the people you know, either. Even if they begin with a real life model, they take on personalities and lives of their own.

People Soup

Another way to use yourself and other real people as characters is to mix them together. Think of creating a recipe for soup:

> Take one person's curly red hair and blue eyes, add another person's sense of humor, and stir in a third person's ability to play basketball. Combine with a fourth person's love of attention. Mix together and place in a school. Let simmer as long as you like. The finished soup is a new character!

You can create soups of your own.

 A. Borrow four ingredients from people you know:

  1. A physical trait from one person.

  2. A personality trait from another.

  3. An ability (or lack of ability!) from a third.

  4. A strong like or dislike from a fourth.

 B. Mix them together. (Describe your new person.)

 C. Place in a setting. (This could be anywhere, a bridge, a tent, an office, or the dark side of the moon.)

 D. Let simmer. (Write as much as you like about what your new person is doing in this place.)

Each set of ingredients is a whole new person, as different from all others as clam chowder is from chicken noodle soup!

Whoppers

If only Pinocchio had been a writer, he wouldn't have had such trouble with his nose! Writers are SUPPOSED to make things up. And it's fun, too!

 A. Tell ten whoppers about yourself. They may be things you wish were true. Or things you're glad aren't true.

  1. Are you a mathematical genius?

  2. A visitor from outer space?

  3. A spy?

  4. Suffering from a dread disease?

  5. The president of a little-known country disguised as a public school student?

  6. Do you have a golden big toe?

  7. Or did a shark eat your big toe?

8. Do you have a secret passageway in the back of your head?

9. Can you hear voices half-way 'round the world—and understand them, no matter what language they're speaking?

The sky's the limit. No fib too big or too small!

B. Once you've got a list of ten whoppers, choose one. You know it's already about a character, because it can't possibly be the real you. Write all about it.

Magic

Sometimes writers are magicians. They create characters out of thin air. Where do THESE characters come from? The imagination. The more you rummage around in your mind, the more characters you'll find there:

Big people, little people, funny people, scary people;
animals, insects, reptiles, fish, and birds;
robots and aliens;
wizards and warlocks;
creatures with flippers or five feet or none.

Reread "Desktop Cleaning," "Mr. Nobody," and "The Attic." Scribbles, cracks in the ceiling, clouds, shadows, and silence are all filled with characters if you let your imagination roam.

What's the difference between creating characters and writing stories? Plot. What happens to the characters? And why? The next two chapters are all about plot.

4

Line Up a Plot

Charlie Brown's day is nothing like Bugs Bunny's day. For one thing, Charlie is a boy and Bugs is a rabbit. But they also have different personalities and interests.

Charlie is timid, awkward, and a worrywart. Nothing ever goes quite right for him. One card on Valentine's Day would be a thrill, but his mailbox is forever empty.

Bugs is outgoing, clever, and daring. He never worries, not even when he's inches away from being made into rabbit stew. He knows he can get himself out of a tight spot as easily as he can get himself into one—and he enjoys doing both.

Charlie Brown would never think of stealing carrots from Elmer Fudd's garden. Bugs Bunny would never stick with a baseball team that couldn't even score one run. Stories told about these characters will always be different from one another.

Certain kinds of characters have certain kinds of adventures. Notice how the main character makes this story happen:

The Dragon Friend
by Rachel Violet Grand
5th grade

There once was a princess whose only wish was to have a dragon friend. She read about dragons, dreamed about dragons, and sometimes ate like a dragon. Now the princess, named Amy, was a sensible girl of ten, and she knew she couldn't have an adult dragon friend for two reasons: number one, the adults were much too big; number two, child dragons had a sense of humor. Adults didn't.

Amy was very sad because she could think of no way to get a baby dragon. Once they were born, they didn't like to leave their mothers.

I know! Amy thought excitedly. I shall get a dragon egg!

She was very pleased with that idea. Then the question occurred to her, "How?" She stewed on that for several days. Finally, she came up with a master plan.

Late that night, she crept out of the castle. Once out, she went to the stable and got her horse, Star. She mounted him and started to ride.

As she rode, she searched for a path that supposedly was there. Suddenly, there it was. There was no doubt in her mind. She turned onto it. Soon, she saw a cave. It glowed from the inside. Amy shivered,

although it was a warm summer night. "Here goes nothing," she said.

She walked into the lair. She touched the cave wall and snatched her hand back. "That wall is hot!" she said.

Soon she saw the dragon. Her heart was beating so hard, she feared the dragon might wake from its deep sleep.

She crept closer. She spied the egg nest. She tiptoed to it, snatched an egg, and ran! She mounted Star and rode as fast as Star could go, back to the castle.

The next morning, Amy awoke with a scaly head on her shoulder. The day-old dragon looked lovingly at Amy. She smiled.

Because of the kind of person Amy is, certain things happen. She's a princess in a make-believe world, so wanting a dragon friend makes sense in her case. Also because of the kind of person she is, she doesn't just sit around hoping, wishing, and dreaming. She sets out to get what she wants.

Suppose your character simply wants a cup of tea. He gets out a teapot, makes the tea, and drinks it. Is that a story? No. Two things are missing. First, what the character wants has to be something truly important, something he or she wants badly enough to take risks to get. Second, that goal can't be too easy to reach. There must be OBSTACLES for the character to fight against.

In "The Dragon Friend," Amy cares enough about dragons to read about them, dream about them, and sometimes even eat like them. But she doesn't just ask for one and get it. She has to face an unfamiliar path late at night, the strange glow and burning walls of the cave, the sleeping dragon, and the fearful hammering of her own heart.

The WANTING gets us interested in the character. The OBSTACLES keep us interested. Will she get what she wants? How? When? If not, why not? And what will she do then? What happens next? The fun of writing and reading stories is in finding out the answers to those questions.

Each of the characters you created in the last chapter has stories to tell. In this chapter and the next, you'll learn two ways to get those stories going.

Here is a plot outline for one type of story. We'll call it Type A.

Scenes are presented in which:

1. a character is introduced who wants something;

2. obstacles come between the character and his or her goal, and he or she struggles to overcome them;

3. a climax is reached, and during this most important struggle with an obstacle, we see that the character either will or will not reach the goal;

4. the effects of the climax are shown and the story ends.

"The Dragon Friend" follows this outline. So does the well-known movie *E.T.* The extra-terrestrial E.T. is left behind when his spaceship leaves Earth. He wants to go home. And it's important that he does go home. If he stays away too long, he'll die.

Many obstacles stand in E.T.'s way. He has no spaceship and no way to communicate with his fellow aliens. He makes friends with three children and will miss them terribly if he goes. Scientists capture him and want to keep him on earth so they can study him.

At last, in an exciting escape scene, E.T.'s young friends help him return to his spaceship and his home planet.

In "The Dragon Friend" and in *E.T.*, the main character gets what he or she wants. But not all Type A stories end happily. Sometimes the main character fails to reach the goal, and the story ends sadly. Sometimes the main character reaches the goal, but finds out it's not what he or she thought it would be. That's what happens in "The Adventure of Ter-Ter."

The Adventures of Ter-Ter
by Beth A. Montgomery
7th grade

Ter-Ter the mutt was out for her morning jog, her brown fur sparkling in the sunlight. Her velvet ears blew gently in the wind as she glided over the paths she had traveled so often. Ter-Ter was rounding the

corner of the barn when she heard screams. They were coming from the cliff above the barn.

Ter-Ter listened intently, debating what to do. She could run and fetch her beloved buddy Ashley, or venture up the cliff alone. The cliff was small, but steep, and Ter-Ter, with her pleasantly plump tummy and tiny paws, was not a skilled climber.

Ter-Ter turned and trotted toward the house. She entered through her dog door and slinked across the kitchen floor and through the hall to Ashley's room, conscious of the paw prints she left behind. She rapped her paw on Ashley's door and hoped for an answer. There was no reply.

Back at the cliff, Ter-Ter stared at the task looming before her. Few trees, bushes, or rocks would make good steps to hop between, and if she fell, she'd land in the pigpen. Her only choice was to follow the cliff from below until it evened with the surrounding farmland.

Ter-Ter rounded a corner of the cliff and galloped along the road. She listened to the pitter-patter of her paws as they hit the cold dirt. She noticed a small trail leading up a steep hill that cornered the cliff and provided an easy and safe way up. Ter-Ter scrambled over the jagged rocks and small bushes that lay in the path. The screams had become fewer and farther between, but could still be heard above the whistle of the wild prairie wind.

Ter-Ter listened to the horrid shrieks. The voice sounded familiar—like Ashley's! The top of the cliff was barren except for a few huge boulders, slightly smaller piles of rocks, clumps of prairie grass, and a few bushes.

The sun was hot on Ter-Ter's furry back; only a few billowy clouds spotted the pale blue sky. Ter-Ter dragged herself under the shadow of a nearby rock, exhausted and panting.

As she rested, she heard the screams again. Then fiendish laughter shattered her train of thought. Yes, those screams were Ashley's, and someone else was with her! Ter-Ter searched behind the rocks, barking and growling ferociously to warn Ashley's fiendish monster.

Ashley was not behind the rocks, and was nowhere else to be found. Ter-Ter was ready to give up when she spotted a small grove of trees. A white napkin was blowing toward her, coming from the direction of the grove. She grabbed it in her snout and ran as fast as her little paws could carry her to the grove. "Ashley, I'm coming to save you!" she tried to shout, but all that came out was a grunt, a few barks, and a muffled howl.

Ter-Ter stopped abruptly once inside the grove. Ashley and several friends were seated on a blanket with the remnants of a picnic spread before them as they screamed with laughter.

"Look!" said Ashley, still laughing. "Ter-Ter wants to eat, too. She even brought a napkin!"

However Type A stories turn out, they all have this in common: The main character wants something badly and

41

tries hard to get it. That's what starts the story rolling and keeps it moving forward.

It's your turn to try a Type A story. Right now, you'll just plan it. Later, in Chapter Six you'll work on the actual writing.

A. Begin at the beginning, with a character who wants something. Check over the characters you discovered in Chapter 3 for some possibilities. Or think about the kinds of things people want:

> friendship
> power
> money
> adventure
> freedom
>> and so on.

What kind of a character might want friendship? Someone lonely? Who might be lonely? A lost child? An elderly person? A newcomer in town? The last person on earth? The first person on Mars?

What kind of person might long for adventure? Someone sickly who can't leave the house? Someone who's grown up in a small town and never traveled? Someone who's read a lot of books about adventure?

Once you've found your character, write a description of him or her. Tell what the goal is, and why your character wants it.

B. Now plan the obstacles. What kinds of things stand between your character and that goal? Basically, there are three kinds of obstacles:

    physical obstacles

    other people

    the character himself or herself

- Ter-Ter faces many *physical* obstacles in getting up that cliff in search of Ashley: the cliff, heat, and the rocks.
- *People* sounds confuse her.
- Her *own* plump tummy and tiny paws make her journey difficult.

    E.T. has to deal with all three kinds of obstacles.

- His separation from his spaceship and the distance from his home planet are *physical* problems.
- The hostility of most of the adults in the movie, especially those who want to capture and study him, are *people* problems.
- His *own* devotion to his new, young friends makes going home even harder for him.

    Write down a list of obstacles your character may have to face. Try to get a few of each kind. You may not use all of them in your final story, but the more you have to choose from, the better off you'll be. The harder your character struggles, the stronger your story will be.

C. Save your biggest, worst, hardest-to-overcome obstacle for last. This will be the one your character has to meet up with in the climax of your story. Why save the worst for last? Because it makes a better story.

    You don't tell the punch line of a joke at the beginning, do you? If you blurt it out too soon, the joke is ruined. There's nothing to look forward to. Once the WORST obstacle in a story is conquered, the rest seem easy— and the suspense is gone.

For now, choose one obstacle that might qualify for the BIG SCENE—the climax of your story. Write it down. You may change your mind when the writing actually gets underway. That's all right. This is only a plan, and plans change.

D. Add a brief ending. Once the punchline of a joke is told, the joke ends. No one wants to hang around to hear it again, or worse yet, listen to the teller explain why it was funny. The same goes for a story. During the climax, we see that the character is either going to get what he or she wants, or not. All we need now is a quick knot to tie everything up.

Notice how soon Ter-Ter's story ends once she finds Ashley. The reader last glimpses her feeling confused and a bit silly. We know she'll get over the surprise in no time, though, and have a happy reunion with Ashley. Beth didn't have to write that out for us. It's obvious. Her ending is quick and to the point.

What will your readers see of the main character as your story comes to a close? Make a note of it.

Now you have an outline of one kind of story plot. It requires a character who wants something. But not all characters do. What then?

5

Line Up Another Plot

Suppose Charlie Brown's team suddenly began to win one game after another. Charlie might become more confident and less shy. What if Elmer Fudd outsmarted Bugs Bunny time and time again? Bugs might have second thoughts about his daredevil ways. We all spend our lives learning and changing and learning and changing some more. Characters do the same.

In "Time for Truth," note how the main character is changed by what happens to her.

Time for Truth
by Tammison Smith
11th grade

Ashley paced the small room from wall to bed and back again. Books, games, and orange, green, and

45

purple stuffed animals stared down at her from all corners. The room belonged to her little half sister. Ashley was visiting her father and his family, as she had every summer for the last six years.

Her father had remarried shortly after her parents' divorce, and now he had a wife, three children, a dog, and a house in the suburbs. Ashley had locked herself in her half sister's room, alone. It was Tuesday, one of the longest days of the week, next to Thursday. Her stepmother worked Mondays, Wednesdays, and Fridays.

Ashley looked at the clock. Two o'clock, three hours until her father got home from work. Three hours also to make peace with her stepmother. Ashley's father had handed her an ultimatum: "This thing between the two of you is tearing me apart, and it's hurting the family. If you can't get along with her, we'll have to stop your visits here. I still want to see you. I will always love you. But this sulking and silence can't go on."

Talks like that usually ended with Ashley in tears and her father quiet and huffy. This one, however, lasted only long enough for him to deliver the statement, fix her with his blue eyes, and leave. It had happened last night, and she was still reeling.

As far as Ashley was concerned, things could go on as they were. And they would. She'll tell me to bug off, she assured herself. Then I can tell Daddy I tried, and that'll be the end of it.

Sure of the disaster ahead, she reached for the doorknob, but stopped short. Resolve disappeared like mist in the afternoon sun. Hot tears filled her eyes and blinded her. Why, she thought, should she be the one to make amends? It wasn't her fault her father had married her mother or divorced her or married her stepmother. Why should she get the job of making it work?

Old warning bells, that since the divorce had protected her from getting hurt, screamed for her attention. They told her her stepmother would be out to get her, to make her feel bad. Why shouldn't she? She didn't like Ashley.

Soon, Ashley saw, it would be too late. Fear would engulf her and she would never face her stepmother. But because of her father, she had to. Steadying herself with deep breaths, she left the room.

The first thing she saw was her stepmother's back. She was sitting straight and tall at the kitchen table, reading the paper. She looked so imposing Ashley almost turned around, but the memory of her father's face kept her going.

"What do you want from me?" she blurted out.

"Excuse me?" Her stepmother looked up from the paper.

"I said, what do you want from me?" Ashley pushed on, afraid if she stopped she wouldn't start again. "Dad said he wanted peace between us, so I thought I'd try." Even if you don't, she thought.

"O.K.," her stepmother said, slowly lowering the paper. "I'll try, too. Come sit down." She patted the chair next to her, stood up, poured some coffee into a cup, and got a Coke from the pantry. Returning

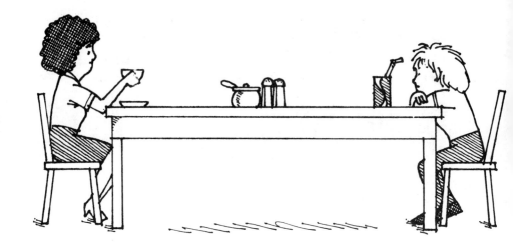

to the kitchen table, she slid the Coke toward Ashley.

"Here," she said. "Where do we start?"

Ashley shrugged, speechless. She fumbled with the tab on the can. Something was wrong. Her stepmother didn't like her; why would she be willing to talk? Ashley's warning bells grew louder. She was being set up for a hard fall. Feeling her stepmother's gaze on her, she opened the Coke with a fizz and let the warm, burning liquid slide down her throat. It brought her voice back.

"I guess we start with what we don't like about each other," she said. What did it matter how they started? It was doomed.

Her stepmother shook her head and said, "I'd rather start with the positive aspects."

Ashley groaned inwardly. Not only did she have to make peace, she had to lie as well.

"I'll start," her stepmother offered. Since Ashley

didn't object, she continued. "I like the way you handle the kids. You tell them stories, make up games, and can always get them to take a bath or go to bed. I get jealous sometimes, you're so good with them." She stopped, looking at Ashley for some sign of recognition.

Ashley nodded, though she was stunned. She never knew her stepmother even noticed her with the kids. Maybe the talk would work out. No, she stopped herself harshly, the bad aspects were still to come.

"Your turn," her stepmother said.

"I like the way you run the house," Ashley found herself admitting. "You manage the work and the budget. I also respect the fact that you're a nurse. I think that's neat."

"Good." Her stepmother stopped to sip her coffee. "Now that we know we don't totally hate each other, maybe we can tell each other some negative aspects of the situation. You first."

Ashley rolled the can between her hands and took another long sip before answering. "I'm not sure how I feel about you," she said. "Even after six years, I hardly know you. My main problem is the feeling I get from you. I feel you don't like me, so I back off." It was the first time she'd admitted that to another person. It made her feel hurt and alone.

Shaking her head, her stepmother took Ashley's hand from the can and said, "Let's get one thing straight. I do like you. You're right that we don't know much about each other. That might be a good place to start." She smiled, wrapped her hands around her cup, and motioned for Ashley to continue.

A bit taken aback, Ashley went on. "Well, I guess I thought you saw me as a threat to your perfect home," she said, retreating behind the Coke and staring at her stepmother over its rim.

She was slowly nodding her head. "I can see where you might get that idea. For a while after your father and I were married, I did see you as a threat. But I came to terms with it, and now I just want to be your friend."

Her last statement nailed Ashley to the chair. Friend! That was a new idea! Ashley realized her stepmother didn't *have* to offer friendship. Maybe she *did* want peace.

"But," her stepmother continued, "I get the same feeling from you that you get from me. I don't think you like me. I have a theory that maybe you blame me for the divorce."

That hurt. The warm feelings Ashley had begun to nurture almost disappeared. Her stepmother had come too close to the truth. Retreating further behind the Coke, Ashley didn't even bother to look at her.

"I thought that was it," her stepmother said. "I'm sorry for what happened, but it's done and you must go on. You can't blame me."

Anger engulfed Ashley. She pushed back her chair, stood up, and yelled at her stepmother: "Yes, I can blame you! You are the one to blame, and the only way it can be fixed is if you leave!"

Hearing her own childish, spiteful words, Ashley blushed furiously and sat down.

"Do you mean that?" her stepmother asked quietly.

"No, I don't think I do," Ashley admitted. "The divorce hurt me a lot, and I needed someone to blame. I loved my parents too much to blame them. You were there, and . . ." Ashley trailed off, helplessly.

Her stepmother smiled and put her hand over Ashley's. "I understand. And I still want to be your friend."

Ashley yanked her hand from her stepmother's grasp. "You don't understand. I think I still blame you. I can never remember a time when my parents weren't fighting. It was better when they split up. I've always known that in my head. But not in my heart. I still don't. I won't be a very good friend to you that way."

"You've voiced your feelings," her stepmother said. "That's a big step toward solving our problem. I want to help." She reached across the table and tipped Ashley's chin up so they met eye to eye. "Will you let me?"

She did want peace. Ashley couldn't deny it. In fact, she had a side to the situation Ashley had never even considered: friendship. Looking through an adult's eyes at her stepmother, Ashley could feel the childish blame that had taken root deep in her heart slip away. Some remained to cushion the truth of her parents' unhappy married life; maybe with time, she could accept that, too. But for now Ashley met her stepmother's steady gaze and asked, "So, where did you grow up?"

In Chapter four, we talked about stories that begin with characters who want something and go after it. But what if your character doesn't want anything? What if, like Ashley at the beginning of this story, he or she would rather not budge, let alone go after a goal? Does that mean that character can never be used in a story?

No, it doesn't. It means that character requires a different kind of story. We'll call this one Type B. It's a harder situation to handle, with the main character refusing to act and threatening to become a bore. But it's not impossible.

In a Type B story, forces enter the main character's life and attempt to make that character change in some way. The forces that change Ashley's life are:

> the divorce
> her father and his last-chance ultimatum
> her stepmother and her offer of friendship
> Ashley's own realization that blaming her step-
>> mother is childish

The outline for this Type B kind of story plot goes like this:

Scenes are presented in which:

1. a character is introduced who is out of step in some way;

2. forces enter the character's life and attempt to change him or her, and the character struggles against them;

3. a climax is reached, in which we see that either the character will have to change or the forces will have to give up;

4. the effects of the struggle are shown and the story ends.

Charles Dickens's Ebenezer Scrooge is just the kind of character I mean. *A Christmas Carol* is a perfect example of a story with a Type B plot.

Scrooge is coldhearted. He doesn't want anything, except money, which he's already got. He'd just as soon the world leave him alone to count it in peace. But the other characters don't want to leave him alone. One after another, they try to FORCE Scrooge to change.

He's asked to donate money to charity. He refuses. His clerk, Bob Cratchit, asks for Christmas Day off from work to be with his family. Scrooge says no. The ghost of his dead partner Marley appears and warns him to change or be sorry. Scrooge ignores the warning. Finally, the ghosts of Christmas past, present, and future appear and lead Scrooge through a nightmarish night until he does, indeed, allow his frozen heart to thaw. We leave him on Christmas morning, buying a goose for the Cratchits' holiday meal, a new and much happier man.

In "Time for Truth" and *A Christmas Carol*, the characters start out with an unpleasant personality trait and the forces are successful in changing that trait.

Sometimes a character has too much of a good personality trait. He or she may be too generous, unable to say no to anyone who asks for a favor. Favor after favor later, that character might finally decide to stand up and say, "NO!" Everyone asking a favor would actually be a force working to change that main character.

Sometimes the forces do their best to change a character, but fail. And sometimes, the forces are WRONG, and the out-of-step character is right not to change. In my story, "The House at the Edge of the City," stubbornness is a trait worth hanging onto.

The House at the Edge of the City

The city is a tall, fast, modern place.

But at its very edge, beside a river, stands a small, yellow house. It belongs to the Merrilees: Grandpa and Grandma, Papa and Mama, Minnie and Max.

One fine spring morning, the mayor of the city paid the Merrilees a call. "Sell me your house," he said "I want to tear it down to make way for new shops."

"Sell our house?" said Grandpa Merrilee.

"Tear it down?" said Grandma.

"Never!" they cried.

And the house stayed, while all the houses to the right of it were torn down to make way for new shops.

"See?" the mayor told the Merrilees. "Your old-fashioned house doesn't belong here anymore."

"It belongs to us," said Grandpa and Grandma. "It belongs just fine."

"You Merrilees," said the mayor, "are stubborn as a tick in a dog's ear. But I will get this house of yours yet."

The Merrilees tended their tulips. They sold just enough flowers to keep their house in good repair and feed and clothe the family.

One sunny summer afternoon, the mayor had a new idea. "Sell me your house," he told the Merrilees. "I want to tear it down to make way for office buildings."

"Sell our house? Tear it down?" said Papa Merrilee. "Never!"

And the house stayed, while all the houses to the left of it were torn down to make way for office buildings.

"See?" said the mayor. "Your old-fashioned house doesn't belong here anymore."

"It belongs to us," said Papa. "It belongs just fine."

"You Merrilees," said the mayor, "are stubborn as a warped door on a wet day. But I will get this house of yours yet."

The Merrilees watered their roses. They sold just enough to keep the house in good repair and feed and clothe the family.

Fall came, and the mayor had another idea. "Sell me your house," he told the Merrilees. "I want to tear it down to make way for apartment buildings."

"Sell our house? Tear it down?" said Mama Merrilee. "Never!"

Once more the house stayed, while all the houses behind it were torn down to make way for apartment buildings.

"See?" said the mayor. "Your old-fashioned house doesn't belong here anymore."

"It belongs to us," said Mama. "It belongs just fine."

The Merrilees minded their mums, and sold just enough to keep their house in good repair and feed and clothe the family. After the first frost, they bedded down their garden for the winter. Then they made popcorn balls and hung them outside on a giant evergreen for all the children who happened by.

One dark, winter evening, the mayor appeared on television. "This is a tall, fast, modern city," he said. "And it is growing taller and faster and more modern every day. The time has come for the Merrilees to sell their house and let us tear it down. It's too old-fashioned. It doesn't belong here anymore. I'm sure you all agree. That's why I'm going to see them again tomorrow morning."

The Merrilees passed a long and gloomy night.

"Could the mayor be right?" Grandma asked Grandpa.

"Should we sell our house?" Grandpa asked Papa.

"Is it really too old-fashioned?" Papa asked Mama.

"Should we let them tear it down?" Mama asked Grandma.

"Sell our house? Tear it down? Never!" said Minnie and Max. But they were small, and no one heard them. So off they went to pay a call on some friends.

When the mayor arrived at the Merrilees' house the next morning, he found children everywhere. And the children had brought their parents and their teachers, their uncles and their aunts, their cousins and their neighbors and their friends.

"Ah," said the mayor, "I see you do agree with me."

"I don't," said a child. "There is no other house like this in the whole city."

"When I was young," said a mother, "there were lots of houses like this. But they were all torn down."

"The Merrilees' house is part of our history," said a teacher.

"But it doesn't belong!" insisted the mayor.

"It belongs to us," said the Merrilees.

"It belongs to us," said the children.

"It belongs to us," said the parents and the teachers, the uncles and the aunts, the cousins, the neighbors, and the friends.

"IT BELONGS JUST FINE!" cried Minnie and Max.

And everyone heard them, even the mayor. "Then keep it," he said, with a sigh. "I have plenty of other ideas."

The city will always be a tall, fast, modern place. But as long as there are Merrilees and flowers, popcorn balls and children, the small, yellow house will still be there.

Type B plots can be as varied as Type A plots, but they all begin in the same way: A character is out of step, and someone or something wants to get that character to change.

Try a Type B plot outline of your own. Again, this is just the planning stage. You'll work on the writing in Chapter six.

A. Begin with an out-of-step character. This time, think of one who's TOO MUCH—

    too cautious,

      too big a daredevil,

        alone too much,

          or too dependent on other people.

Look over the characters you worked on in Chapter three for possibilities. Don't forget to check the interview you did with yourself. You can take one of your traits and "branch out." Suppose, for instance, you like computer games. Your character may be ADDICTED to computer games. Suppose you sometimes feel jealous of a friend. Your character may be CONSUMED by jealousy.

Or consider the six things you don't like to do. Are there forces that try to get you to do them? Do you dig in your heels and resist? Can you branch out from yourself to a character in a similar fix? The trait may be mild at first and get worse as the forces grow stronger. That's one way to develop an exciting plot.

Decide on one character and describe him or her. Be sure to mention the out-of-step trait.

B. Now consider the forces. Who or what might come into this character's life and try to change it? Remember the three kinds of obstacles we talked about in the Type A plot? Forces also come in threes:

life forces,
   forceful people,
      and inner forces.

In *A Christmas Carol,*

- Christmas Eve is a life force that plays its part in changing Scrooge. That holiday has a power all its own.
- Bob Cratchit, his son Tiny Tim, and even the ghosts are examples of people forcing Scrooge to change.
- Scrooge's own hidden feelings eventually come out and help him begin his life anew.

In "Time for Truth,"

- Divorce is a life force working to change Ashley.
- Her father and stepmother are forceful people.
- Because she's growing up, she's able to see the situation differently, and that helps her to change.

Life forces may take the shape of something physical, like a hurricane or drought. They may also be anything new in a character's life, whether it's good or bad. Any change in a person's life is a force that may change that person.

A death in the family makes everyone see life differently.

So does the birth of a baby.

A move to a new town,
   an illness,
      a fire,
         a pet,
            a flunking grade
               or an A+

may also force characters to rearrange their lives and personalities.

People are always at work trying to force other people to change:

    teachers,

      coaches,

        band directors,

          parents,

brothers,
    sisters,
        friends,
            rivals,
                and tv commercial actors
play a game of tug-of-war with all of us.

And if you've ever known anyone on a diet, you know how people can be their own force for change, while their hunger is a completely opposite inner force!

Make a list of all the possible forces that might act to change your character: life forces, forceful people, and inner forces. Again, you may not need all of them when it comes time to write your story. But you'll want to choose the best from a good supply.

C. Save your biggest, strongest, most powerful force for last. This is the climax. What if Cratchit had asked for Christmas Day off and Scrooge had said, "Oh, you poor guy! It never crossed my mind you'd like to be with your family. Sure, go on home." *A Christmas Carol* would have been a short and not terribly interesting tale!

Dickens knew well-told stories build UP, not down. He began with the charity-seekers, then moved on to Cratchit, then to Marley, then to the ghosts. Even with the ghosts, he saved the most important—the future— for last.

In "Time for Truth" the last and most effective force is Ashley's own voice, blaming her stepmother. When Ashley hears how childish it sounds, she knows she has to change.

In "The House at the Edge of the City," the mayor

thinks HE has the last and strongest force: the support of the entire city. But he's wrong!

Choose one of the forces you wrote down for the climax of your story. Make a note to yourself about why THIS one deserves to be in the biggest scene of all.

D. Round off your ending. Once the last and greatest force has its chance to work on your character, there's no ammunition left. Either your character will change— or not. To end his story, and to show change has occurred, Dickens shows Scrooge buying a goose and heading for the Cratchits' Christmas dinner. Ashley asks her stepmother, "So, where did you grow up?" And the mayor gives in to the Merrilees.

What will your character do? Write it down. Your Type B story is lined up and ready to go.

6

Show; Don't Tell

Have you ever gotten so caught up in a terrific book, you began to think the world inside that book was the real one? If, in the middle of your reading, someone called your name, it took you by surprise. Maybe you even jumped up, wondering where you were and what you were supposed to be doing. At the very least, it took you a few seconds to figure out that THIS was the real world, and the one you were reading about was not.

How do writers pull us into their imagined worlds like that? Is it a trick? You could call it that. Or you could call it a technique, a part of the writer's craft. Either way, it's no secret. The technique is nicknamed SDT. Sounds like a bug spray, doesn't it? It isn't. SDT means "Show; don't tell."

Suppose someone invites you to dinner. "Oh, you're going to love what we're having!" that person tells you. "It's the best dish in the world."

Well, you know there will be some kind of food, and your host is excited about it, but what will it be? Are you going to love it just because your host said you would? Or are you going to wait and see what actually gets served?

Some people love caviar—salty fish eggs.

Some people love raw hamburger meat. It's called steak tartare, and it's served with a raw egg on top.

Some people love seaweed.

And some don't.

Saying "It's the best dish in the world" is TELLING. Putting that dish right out there on the table is SHOWING. It's the same whether you cook or write.

ACTION is one way of *showing* rather than *telling*. It brings a scene to life right in front of your reader's eyes.

Here's a "telling" sentence:

She was angry.

Does it make you see anything?

No, there's nothing to see and no one to care about. Somewhere, someone is angry, and we've been told about it. So what?

But look at this "showing" scene:

She kicked open the screen door, letting it slam against the wall as she dashed outside. Down the steps and into the yard she flew. Grabbing the first rock in her path, she hurled it back toward the house. It crashed through the living room window with an explosion of shattered glass.

Now you can see! Not once in that paragraph did I use the word "anger," but you knew that's what it was because you were right there, watching it happen.

DIALOGUE is another way of SHOWING.

Listen to this:

Dad and I disagreed about everything. We were always arguing.

Hear anything?

Nope. Whatever these two are arguing about is too far away. We're all familiar with fathers, and we've been in an argument or two. But we really don't know what's going on here, so it's hard to feel sympathetic.

Listen again:

"Dad, I can handle it," I said. "Ten hours a week at a job is just a couple of hours a day."

Dad put down his coffee cup and glared at me. "I said no job," he insisted. "You have your whole life to work. Or bum around with a band, if that's what you want to do. Right now, you study."

"I *do* study," I told him. "And I *will* study. I promise I won't let my grades slip. But that band is starting up *now*. I need that new snare drum *now*. I'm not even asking you to buy it for me. All I want is—"

Dad's fist hit the tabletop. "No job!" he shouted. "And no band! School comes first. And that's that!"

Hear anything now? I should think so! You've got a front row seat. And you have a clear picture of when and how these two argue and what about.

Sensory images are a third way of showing.

Picture this:

Her room was a mess.

Mean anything to you?

Well, maybe. Most of us can picture a messy room. The trouble is the messy room I was thinking of when I wrote that sentence is not the same one you thought of when you read it.

Who's fault is that? Mine. I TOLD you about a messy room. I didn't SHOW you which one I meant.

So, *picture this*:

The needle stuck, trapping Bruce Springsteen in mid-shout, a kind of "wuh-huh, wuh-huh, wuh-huh" sound. On and on it went. Rick pounded on the wall and called his sister's name, but nothing stopped it.

He tried the doorknob. At first the door wouldn't budge. He pushed harder and managed to inch it forward. Peering through the crack, he realized a mound of jeans and tattered sweatshirts had formed a barricade holding the door shut. He could smell them, and sneakers, too, the unmistakeable aroma of locker room sweat.

Shoulder to the task now, he managed to work his way inside. The spicy aroma of pepperoni pizza rose above the sneakers to tickle his nose and tongue. A cardboard box, empty except for a sprinkling of crumbs, lay atop a tangle of blankets on the bed.

Rick picked his way over the smelly clothes, a tennis racket, and a gaping gym bag. Edging around the dresser, he whacked his shin on an open drawer. But the rest was easy. Only a few textbooks, pencils, a calculator, and wads of notebook paper lay between him and the stereo in the corner. He set Bruce free.

"Peggy?" he whispered into the sudden silence. "Peggy, are you in here?" No answer. It's finally happened, he thought. The mess has swallowed her up whole.

NOW you're right where I want you, inside the exact

room I wanted to SHOW you. How did I get you there?
I invited you in by each of your five senses:

sight
sound
taste
touch
smell

Like insects with antennae vibrating, we're constantly running checks, through our senses, on what's out there around us and what's in here, inside our own bodies. Are we well? Are we safe? Watch out for that car! Do I smell hot chocolate? Was that thunder?

If we lose one sense or two, we can usually do all right with those that are left. But what if we had none at all? We'd have no idea where we left off and the furniture began.

We experience the real world through our five senses, and we experience fictional worlds in the exact same way. The more a writer helps us see, hear, taste, touch, and smell an imagined world, the more real that world becomes.

Most of the time we run our sensory checks on the real world and ourselves without thinking much about them. The sky turns gray, a dog barks, a honeysuckle vine blooms, and we barely notice. Occasionally, a car accident, a parade, or a rainbow comes along and makes us stop and PAY ATTENTION. But not often—unless we want to write and lure our readers into the worlds we're writing about.

A writer has to practice paying attention. Here are a few ways to do just that. They'll help you gather action, dialogue, and sensory images to use in your stories.

Action

A. This is a list of common, everyday actions:
    a wink
    a shrug
    a sneer

a tapping foot
an elbow nudge
biting one's lip
a wave of the hand
a pat on the back
holding hands
a slap
a jump

A wink might mean a secret is passing between two people. Or it might mean the winker has something in his eye. What else could a wink show?

A pat on the back might encourage someone to try harder. Or it might save someone from choking to death. What else?

Think of the many different ways each of these actions could be used to SHOW something. Then add other actions to your list and come up with uses for them. Don't stop with the first thing that comes to mind. Keep looking for more and more ways to put those actions to work.

B. Now, here's a list of common, everyday feelings:
love
grief
anger
fear
joy
jealousy
boredom

What actions do people use to SHOW these feelings? What actions might you use if you were in a play and had to show the audience how your character felt?

Make a list of actions for each emotion. Think of both

common and uncommon actions. We've already seen "throwing rocks" as a way of showing anger, but some people burst into tears when they're angry. Make as long a list for each emotion as you can, then list other emotions and do the same for them.

Now when you find yourself writing a "telling" statement like, "She was angry," you can find ways to SHOW your readers exactly what you mean.

Dialogue

You use dialogue every day. Try writing some.
A. Picture a family gathering for dinner. There are four people. You decide who they are. It could be a grandparent, a parent, and two children. Or a parent and three children. Or two parents, a child, and a guest. Or any other combination you choose. List your four characters by name, relationship, and age, like this:

> Don Green, father, forty-three
> Melissa Green, his daughter, fourteen
> Bob Green, Melissa's brother, ten
> Larry Brown, Bob's friend, ten

Now give your reader information about these characters using nothing but dialogue. Don't worry about the "he said" and "she said" part right now. Concentrate on the dialogue itself.

Here's an example:

Question: What are the names of your characters?

(THINK: What might your characters SAY to get those names across to the reader?)

DON: Bob! Melissa! Time for dinner. Hurry up.

BOB: Coming, Dad. Is it okay if Larry eats with us?

DON: Oh, hi, Larry. Sure, join us.

LARRY: Thanks, Mr. Green.

Just by talking to each other in a natural way, these characters have revealed all four of their names.

Now you try it. Remember to use dialogue only. And don't worry about writing a complete story. Just give the information asked for.

1. Write dialogue revealing the names of YOUR characters.

2. Write dialogue that tells where the characters are and what they're doing. (Example: "Are you going to eat dinner in front of the TV again?")

3. Write dialogue that tells something personal about these people. (Example: "This is the third time we've had macaroni and cheese this week. I'm beginning to feel like a rat.")

4. Have one character make an important announcement that takes the others by surprise. Make it something that will change their lives. (Example: "I've got a new job. We're moving to Texas.")

5. Write dialogue in which at least two of the characters argue about the news. See if you can't get all of them into the discussion. Make sure each person who talks has his or her own point of view. Each speaker should have something different to say and, most importantly, his or her own way of saying it. (Example: "You mean I have to change schools?" "What about the dog, huh, Dad? Huh?")

Don't worry about finishing the argument or straightening everything out. This isn't a complete story. But it might grow into one.

B. Practice writing dialogue by coming up with scenes of your own. Any place where two or more people get together and talk will do:

a club meeting
a ball game
a party or dance
a swimming pool
a grocery store
an elevator
a parking lot

The information asked for in Part A can be used in almost any situation to get those people talking. After that, come up with more and better things for them to discuss on your own. You'll find the more they talk, the more they'll come to life for you. They'll begin to tell you stories.

Sensory Images

A. Try this five-minute practice session:

Find a place, indoors or out, where you can be alone and undisturbed for five minutes. Settle in comfortably and concentrate on your senses. Give each of them one full minute. Don't take notes. Just notice.

1. What do you see? Look up and down as well as around.

2. What do you hear? Listen for the tiny sounds along with the loud ones.

3. What do you smell? Even if nothing's cooking, there's always a smell of some kind. Search for it.

4. What do you taste? You're not eating, you say? That's all right. Your tastebuds aren't asleep. Even the air has a taste, and it's different on hot, humid days than on cold, crisp days.

5. What are you touching? Close your eyes and concentrate on how things FEEL.

6. After five minutes, write down your observations. You may find you've noticed more in those five minutes than you sometimes notice in a whole day!

B. Each time you visit a new place, take five minutes to observe it, one sense at a time. Then write about it.

C. Once you've gotten the hang of paying attention to your senses and writing down the information they've gathered for you, try using that information in fiction.

1. Spend a good five-minute session alone with your senses—and no writing at all. Then get out your notepad.

2. Create a character who's completely alone. It might be a hermit,
   or a lost astronaut,
      or a prisoner,
         or hiker on a mountainside.

It's up to you. Describe your character and his or her situation.

3. Have your character suddenly recall the five minutes YOU just spent observing things as if those five minutes were part of the character's own past, a memory that suddenly came back.

73

As you write, use those sensory details you took such care to notice.

4. Link your character's sudden memory with his or her present state of being completely alone. Why did this memory pop up? Why now? What does it mean to this character?

What you have written isn't a story, although it may be part of one. But it is a good way to practice using your own experiences to fill the world of your stories.

Action, Dialogue, and Sensory Images

Can you work all your SDT muscles at once? Bring the following dull examples of TELLING to life by SHOWING through action, dialogue, and the five senses. You may not use every technique each time. It's up to you to pick and choose the most effective details for each scene.

1. The storm was frightening.
2. He really loves basketball.
3. The kid was a brat.
4. Nothing I did went right.
5. He's always showing off.
6. She was so nice to me.
7. Our cafeteria's food is awful.
8. He really looks bad.
9. They ate like pigs.
10. This place is a dump.

Go back to one of your story outlines now. An outline is a lot like TELLING the story, isn't it? This happens

and then that happens and so on. That's fine for you, the writer. You can picture all the details, because you're the one making them up. But it's not nearly enough for your readers. They can't read your mind!

As you begin to write your story, take it scene by scene. At each point in your outline, stop and think:

How can I bring this scene to life for my readers?

Action? (What are my characters doing?)

Dialogue? (What are they saying?)

The five senses? (What do they see, hear, taste, touch, smell?)

How can I SHOW, not tell?

7

Fine-Tune Each Sentence

Although writing is more difficult than talking, it does have advantages. One of these is rewriting. Once you've said something, you can't unsay it. It's out there, for better or worse. Even if you correct it by saying something new, the first words have still been heard.

Writing can be erased. It can be crumpled up and thrown away. It can be locked up in a diary or hidden behind your old sneakers at the back of a closet. It can also be rewritten and rewritten again until it's ready to be shared with readers.

Have you ever had an argument with someone and twenty minutes later, when you were alone, thought of all the things you SHOULD have said? Oh, you could have told that someone off GOOD! Too late now. Or maybe you wished you HADN'T said this or that. Why didn't you just keep your big mouth shut? Too late for that, too.

It's never too late to rewrite a story. There's plenty of time to add all the terrific stuff you think of AFTER the first try. Take that time to rethink your story, with rewriting in mind.

You've begun with an outline, an overview of what will happen and when and why and to whom.

You've brought that story and its characters to life by showing instead of telling. You've come up with scenes that use action, dialogue, and the five senses to get your ideas across to the reader.

Now check the words you've chosen. Are they behaving the way you want them to? Or have they run wild?

How do you know when words are behaving? They get right to work and they get the job done. This haiku is a good example:

Monarch Butterfly
by Rhonda A. Lee
7th grade

Monarch butterfly
soars through the air lightly. Now
rests on a grass blade.

Only thirteen words, seventeen syllables, but a lot of work is being done here. First, there's the picture presented. From the moment the poem begins, we know what we're looking at: a monarch butterfly. We can see its orange and black coloring.

With that set in our minds, we can watch it soar. Butterflies do many things when they fly: flit, flutter, flip, flicker. This one soars, a straight, strong line of flight. Not like a jet plane, though. It soars *lightly*. And then it rests. Not just anywhere, but on a single blade of grass.

The words *show* us exactly what's happening. Because they're well-chosen and hard-working, they also give us more to think about than the physical picture. This flight that ends on one blade of grass is delicate and brief. Butterflies are delicate, and their lives are brief.

Notice that tiny word "now" all alone at the end of the second line. "Later will be too late," it says. "Look NOW." Many beautiful things in nature are fragile and pass quickly. We need to enjoy them while we can.

The more we think about them, the harder these words work. Poetry, like this haiku, is often beautiful and brief—like the flight of a butterfly. It soars for a moment, then comes to rest in each reader's mind and heart. Everything I've said is MY response to this poem. Your reactions may be entirely different. So the words work on and on and on each time they meet a new reader.

All of those ideas were packed into seventeen syllables! Well-trained words are rich in meaning.

Because poems are usually shorter than stories, poets have more time to worry over each sound and syllable. Story writers, with thousands of words to juggle, can't always be as fussy. But we can learn a lot from the poet's attention to precise, hard-working words.

Lazy,
   out of place,
   and show-off words
have no place in any kind of writing.

Lazy Words

Some lazy words have been worked so hard, they're worn out. What does "love" mean, for instance, when someone can say,
   "I love you, Mom,"
      and "I love chocolate,"
         and "I love your new shoes,"
and mean all three statements?

Does the speaker feel the same about her mother, a pair of loafers, and a Hershey bar? If not, how DOES she feel? The true meaning of a word is anybody's guess when that word has been overused until it's worn out.

Other lazy words just don't have what it takes to stay on the job very long. Years ago, "You're the cat's pajamas" was a compliment, but it would be an odd thing to say now. Words like "cool," "dude," "wimp," and "nerd" soar for a while, but unlike that butterfly, when they land, it's with a THUD.

The latest language fads are fun when you're talking to friends. But when you take the trouble to write a story, you want it to last longer than a conversation. So avoid slang. You'd be surprised at how quickly it can make what you've written sound out-of-date.

There are lazy words that just take up space.

It was a pretty good party. Everyone had a pretty nice time. The food was pretty good, too. So was the music.

What does "pretty" mean here? Is a pretty good party a good party? Or is it a bad party? It's impossible to tell.

"Hey! That's pretty good!" often means "That's good!"

"Well, it was pretty good," can mean "That should have been better."

"It was pretty good, I guess," can be a polite way of saying, "I hated it."

Watch out for other space-gobbling lazy words:

> very
> really
> a little
> a lot
> rather
> somewhat
> sure
> much

Does this mean you may never use any of these words? Of course not. Use them when they're needed, not when they creep in for no good reason. They SURE take up A LOT OF space, but they don't REALLY add MUCH meaning. (Read that sentence without the capitalized words, and you'll see.)

Some lazy words repeat themselves. Careless repetition, as with all those "pretty" words above, is boring. Repetition can be effective, though. Here's an example:

Spiders
by Patrick Colvand
6th grade

I like spiders
    black spiders
    mean spiders
    poison spiders
    ugly spiders
Any kind of spider
    a spider on my arm
    a spider on my pants
    a spider on my sleeve
    a spider eating ants
I like spiders
    round spiders
    dumb spiders
    squashed spiders
    smart spiders
    bloody spiders
    dead spiders
I like spiders.

It's obvious Patrick hasn't let in any lazy spiders. The repetition is there on purpose, for the fun of it. It's fun to come up with all kinds of spiders—and it's fun to recite them, especially to people who don't like them!

Lazy words in lazy sentences run on forever. Unplanned repetition may cause perfectly fine words to go bad.

He went outside and he looked around, but he didn't see anyone, so he went back inside, and then he poured himself a glass of lemonade and he . . .

Short lazy sentences that bump along in non-stop spurts are no better:

He went outside. He looked around. He didn't see anything. He went back inside. He poured himself a glass of lemonade. He . . .

There's a time for long sentences and a time for short sentences. Think about what sentence length does to a story. Long sentences tend to slow the action down. They're perfect for describing quiet moments, like a stroll through a peaceful woodland setting.

Short sentences speed things up. They make us tense. No time to waste. Let's hit the road. Move it.

A mixture of short and long words, sentences, and paragraphs will add variety and interest to your story.

Lazy nouns and verbs cannot be pepped up by adjectives and adverbs. Note how an army of adjectives can't help the vague noun "animal" in this sentence:

I saw an animal.
I saw a big animal.
I saw a big, wide animal.
I saw a big, wide, wrinkled animal.
I saw a big, wide, wrinkled, gray animal.
Okay! Okay! BUT WHAT WAS IT?
I saw an elephant.
OH! Why didn't you SAY so?
Lazy verbs get into similar trouble:
She ran home quickly.
No, that's not right.
She ran home very quickly.
That's not it, either.
She ran home rapidly.
No.
She ran home briskly.
Nope.
She ran home quite briskly.
Uh-uh.
She ran home quite briskly and very rapidly.
No! No! No!

"Ran" is not working here. And when the verb is wrong, adverbs can't make it right. We have other verbs to choose from, and each has a slightly different meaning. Did she dash? Bolt? Trot? Gallop? Fly?

No. She *raced* home.

That's it! At last!

Many people think fancy adjectives and adverbs are what writing is all about. But that's the lazy way out. Careful writers turn first to hard-working nouns and verbs.

The monster reared up on its hind legs and staggered toward us. Its eyes never left my face. Drops of its last victim's blood fell from the claws of its raised right paw. In its left paw, it clutched a pickle.

Was that meant to be a suspenseful passage? Or a funny one? It started out suspensefully, but "pickle" turned it around.

"Pickle" is a funny word. I don't know why. Maybe because it rhymes with "tickle." Maybe because it's associated with things that are fun, like picnics and potato chips and hot dogs. Whatever the reason, one thing is for sure: If you're trying to write a serious or

suspenseful or scary scene, hold the dills. Let the monster clutch a rock or a tree limb.

Wiggle and giggle and jiggle are funny words. Slither isn't.

A snake that wiggles through the grass isn't nearly as threatening as one that slithers.

"Lilac" and "lullaby" are lovely words.

"Buzzard" is beastly.

The sounds of words can add to their meaning.

But "The lovely lilac languished on the lemon linoleum" gets on our nerves. Enough! we cry. No matter how much you like pepper, you wouldn't blacken your scrambled eggs with it. A little goes a long way, with both spices and sounds.

Show-Off Words

When you set out to write a story, you didn't say, "I think I'll write some fabulous words." You had characters in mind, and a plot, and a setting. You knew you'd need words, but you never intended for them to take over.

When individual words and phrases show off, they stop blending into meaningful sentences and paragraphs. They grab the reader's attention and push the story into the background.

Watch for the show-off words in this exchange of dialogue. Actually, you don't have to watch for them. You won't be able to miss them!

"Hi!" she exclaimed, eagerly.

"How are you?" he interrogated.

"I'm fine," she vocalized. "How are you?"

"Furious," he fumed, angrily.

This simple conversation is lost in a forest of show-off words. Compare that with these well-trained words:

"Hi!" she said.

"How are you?" he asked.

"I'm fine," she said. "How are you?"

"Furious," he replied.

Notice how the dialogue gets all the attention now?

If dialogue is well-written, it's perfectly capable of telling the reader what he or she needs to know. There's no need to explain it in the tag lines. They're just there to identify the speaker. Someone who announces that he's "furious" is obviously angry. How else would he say "Furious" except angrily?

Dialogue isn't the only thing that can be overshadowed by show-off words. Readers don't mind an occasional unfamiliar term. In fact, it's fun to learn a new word now and then. You can usually figure out its meaning from its place in the sentence, so it doesn't distract you for long.

On the other hand, no one enjoys keeping one eye on the dictionary while the other struggles through a story.

> "A singularity, *Solanium tuberosum,*
> a duplication, *Solanium tuberosum,*
> a triumvirate, *Solanium tuberosum,*
> a quaternity"

is certainly an impressive batch of words, but it will never replace

> "One, potato,
> two, potato,
> three, potato,
> four."

Just because a word is unusual or has more than one syllable doesn't make it a better word. An enormous, obese, herbivorous pachyderm is still the long way 'round an elephant. There are times, though, when "enormous" is better than "big" and when "herbivorous" is exactly what you mean to say. In that case, say it.

Similes and metaphors can draw your readers closer to your story. But they can be show-offs, too, especially when used too often.

Similes and metaphors compare the unfamiliar to the familiar, so that the unfamiliar is easier to understand.

For example: You want to tell your reader that a car ride through a particular area was hot and dry. The reader is unfamiliar with that area and how it looks and feels, but knows what a desert is, so you compare the two. A simile uses "like" or "as." A metaphor doesn't.

Simile: The drive through Bart's Pass in mid-August was like a long day in the desert.

Metaphor: The drive through Bart's Pass in mid-August was a long day in the desert.

Either way, your reader pictures a vast, hot, dry, barren landscape with a blazing sun overhead and no relief in sight. You've gotten your setting across quickly and effectively.

Remember those peppered scrambled eggs? Too many similes and metaphors can be just as bad:

The car was as steamy as a hot shower on a cold day. The food we'd packed smelled like garbage cans left too long in the sun. Sweat dribbled down my back like a thousand centipedes headed south.

Soon the reader is so busy picturing hot showers,

garbage cans, and centipedes, the car driving through Bart's Pass in mid-August is totally forgotten.

Words, phrases, sentences, paragraphs—even letters and sounds—have one job: to keep the story rolling. Wild words can break a story down. Well-trained words fine-tune it.

Get to know new words and have fun with them. Make a list of them in your journal: list funny ones and scary ones, sad ones and odd ones.

Practice using nouns and verbs that can stand on their own. Add adjectives and adverbs only when needed.

Play around with similes and metaphors. Which are your own, original inventions and which are cliches you've heard over and over?

Try out a variety of sentence lengths. Break down paragraphs and see how they look rearranged.

Then choose what's best for the story you're writing. Even if "confiscable" is your favorite word in the whole world, if it doesn't fit THIS STORY, weed it out, along with any others that are lazy, out of place, or showing off.

8

Pass the Final Inspection

Writers learn to write by writing. You can talk about it, read about it, and dream about it, but none of that is quite the same as doing it.

Writers also learn to write by studying the work of other writers, both professional and beginners. Read all the published stories and books you can. Think about the ones you like and what you like about them. Think about the ones you don't like—and what went wrong.

Read the stories your friends write. Share your work with those who care as much about writing as you do: friends, teachers, parents. You can learn from their opinions about what you've written, and from your own opinions about what THEY'VE written.

This chapter will give you guidelines for getting the most out of rereading and editing your own stories and those other people have written and shared with you.

Every story you've ever seen in print has been read by at least one editor, and often more than one. This is true whether that story was by a beginner or by an experienced writer with dozens of stories to his or her credit. It's also true of novels, plays, poems, articles—and this book.

Those editors have offered the writer suggestions about how to make that story—one the editor already thought was good enough to publish—even better. Truly professional writers welcome those suggestions, even though they mean more work. Often the writer has to rewrite several times before the story is ready to go to press.

Why?
If the writer began with a good idea,
and knew how to create characters,
and how to outline a plot,
and how to show rather than tell,
and how to fine-tune his or her story,
why wasn't the story already perfect?

Think of it this way:

If I asked you to hold a baseball bat correctly, you could do it;

if I asked you to hold a lighted candelabra, you could do that, too;

if I asked you to hold a live chicken, you could even do that.

But what if I asked you to juggle a baseball bat, a lighted candelabra, and a live chicken? That's the difference between learning the basics of story writing and putting them all together into a story.

It takes practice. But even after years of practice, each new story, like each toss of those three items, is a new challenge. The most experienced among us sometimes drops the bat, or a candle, or the chicken. And we may not even notice.

We're so busy with a difficult character, we let the fine-tuning slip. Or we get so involved with fine-tuning the words, we forget part of the plot. Or we struggle so to get the climax as exciting as possible, we bend a character out of shape.

Editors, teachers, and other writers can spot where we've gone wrong. They can even suggest ways to make the juggling act more spectacular, something that's hard to think about when you're the one madly juggling.

And you can help your friends who write, even when they're making the exact same mistakes you are! It's odd, but true, that it's easier to see a mistake when somebody else is making it. If you're really alert, you can apply what you teach other writers to your own work and improve it even more:

Notice how Jim never mentions what his main character looks like? Did you?

See how Jane tells too much of her story instead of showing it? How about you?

Did Jeff rush right through the climax of his story in a sentence or two? Is he the only one?

Writing can be very personal. It's not easy to share. Beginners get discouraged if friends don't like their stories. Experienced writers get discouraged if critics disapprove of theirs. A few simple rules, though, can make sharing your work more pleasant and more useful.

Rules for Sharing Your Work

1. Respect your craft.

Musicians don't perform songs they've never rehearsed or play on out-of-tune instruments. Writers perfect and double-check their spelling, grammar, and punctuation. They present their work clearly written or typed on clean paper.

2. Get your story in shape before you show it around.

It's not fair to others to ask them to judge unwritten ideas, half-finished stories, or rough first drafts. They simply won't have enough information to go on.

It's not fair to you, either. A harsh judgment given too soon may keep you from going on. Too much praise may encourage you to talk the rest of your story away.

Hang onto the feeling of having a terrific secret and no way to share it except by writing every bit of it down.

3. Judge words on a page, not the person who wrote them.

Kind and generous people have been known to write poorly. Nasty people are capable of writing well. And nice people who are also fine writers often make mistakes.

Written mistakes can be fixed fairly easily. Hurt feelings can't. When someone is reading your work, tell yourself that's what it is: words on paper, not you. When you're reading someone else's work, make sure that person understands this basic rule. "This sentence is confusing," does NOT mean, "You're a terrible writer and a worthless human being." All it means is, "This sentence is confusing."

4. An editor's goal is to help the writer make his or her story as good as it can be, *not* to get that writer to write a different story.

If your reader makes a suggestion you like, use it.

If you absolutely disagree, don't use it.

But be open-minded. An idea may sound hopeless at first, but give it a chance. Think it over. A day or two later, it may begin to make sense.

If you make a suggestion about someone else's work and that person disagrees, be gracious. It's not your story. You can always write one of your own *your* way!

To evaluate a story fairly, you'll need to read it at least twice. The first time, read it straight through. Simply enjoy it. The second time, go through it slowly and carefully. Measure it against the following guidelines.

   A. Idea
     1. What is the main idea of this story? What point is the writer trying to make?
     2. Is it an interesting idea?
     3. Is the main idea clear to you? Or are you left

wondering at the end, "What was that all about"?

B. Characters
  1. Who is the main character? Can you tell?
  2. Is the main character someone the reader can understand and care about?
  3. Does the main character stay "center stage?" Do we follow him or her through the entire story—or do others keep grabbing the spotlight?
  4. Are there too many characters? Too few?
  5. Do the characters seem real and believable?
  6. Are they described so that you can "see" them?
  7. By the end of the story, do you feel you know them?
  8. Are you glad you met them?

C. Plot
  1. If this is a Type A plot, does the main character want something important enough to keep you interested in whether he or she will get it?
  2. If this is a Type B plot, is the main character's out-of-step trait clear? Can you understand what forces want to change that trait and why? Does the situation capture your interest?
  3. Are the obstacles or forces strong enough to make the plot suspenseful? Or are they pushovers? Do they get stronger and more difficult as the story moves along?
  4. Is the climax the story's most dramatic scene? Is it shown in full detail?

5. Does the ending satisfy you? Does it make sense? Does everything fit together naturally? Or are there too many coincidences, lucky breaks, or unlikely last-minute rescues?

D. Show; Don't Tell
   1. Are the characters shown living their story through action and dialogue?
   2. Does the story involve your senses? Can you see, hear, smell, taste, and touch what's going on?
   3. Or does the narrator seem to be reporting back to you from a place you never get to visit first-hand?
   4. Is there a balance in the use of action, dialogue, and the five senses? Or does the story stop too often for the smell of every flower and the taste of every french fry and the feel of each pebble along the way?

E. Fine Tuning
   1. Are there lazy words and worn-out words that could be replaced with words that work harder?
   2. Is there too much repetition? Are there words, phrases, or passages that could be cut out?
   3. Has the writer used strong nouns and verbs? Or are weak choices being propped up by too many adjectives and adverbs?
   4. Are the similes and metaphors effective? Are they overdone? Are any of them clichés you've heard too often?

5. Do out-of-place words and show-off words jump out at you as you read along?
6. Is there variety in the lengths of words, sentences, and paragraphs?
7. Are there mistakes in grammar, punctuation, or spelling?

These guidelines won't apply equally to every story you write or read. You'll have to use your own judgment in deciding which points are important in improving which stories. But EVERY TIME you read another writer's story and EVERY TIME someone reads yours (even if that someone is YOU), see that these two bits of business get done:

• Tell what you LIKE about the story. Be sure to mention every positive aspect you've found. This isn't just being polite. With one eye on the baseball bat, one eye on the candelabra, and one eye (a third eye?) on the chicken, we can easily miss mistakes—but we can just as easily miss what's going well. Point it out!

• Ask every question about the story that occurs to you. Ask the questions in the guidelines, but also ask about whatever you don't understand,
   whatever you'd like to know more about,
   whatever bothers you in any way.
The more you THINK about a story
   and EXAMINE it
   and QUESTION it,
the more you will learn about improving that story and writing the next one and the one after that.

9

What's In it for You?

Everyone has stories to tell. Children too young to read tell stories. Liars make them up and pretend they're true. Cave dwellers illustrated theirs on the walls of caves.

Daydreamers tell stories to themselves. So do writers. Most of the time, we plan to share what we've written, but not always. And before we think of sharing, we write for ourselves.

Why do we do it? Why spend hours at a typewriter or computer, or pen in hand, telling stories with no one there to listen? What do we get out of it? Plenty.

• We write to help ourselves think straight.

When life gets frantic, or frightening, or upsetting in any way, thoughts tend to jumble. Words on a page stand still. They wait for us to calm down. They can be rearranged to make better sense out of what's happened.

• We write to keep track of who we are.

Spoken words come and go. What's written down lasts. Each person's ideas and ideals are part of the story of humanity. They're of interest to each of us, looking back on them ten or twenty or fifty years later. They're of interest to our families and friends, too—and maybe to the stranger who happens upon our words clear across the continent or long after we're gone.

• We write to take a break from real life.

When we need to escape for a while, stories, like daydreams, are a place to go. They're a vacation in another world, all expenses paid. No reservations needed.

• We write to keep us out of trouble.

Anger, jealousy, revenge, and other negative feelings can get us into trouble in real life. Or they can provide the drama that makes a story exciting. Toss wicked witches into the oven. Bash bloodthirsty ogres with their own clubs. Wrestle dragons, slay tyrants, embarrass selfish stepsisters with big, fat, ugly feet. No one gets hurt. No one need ever know.

• We write to live better lives.

Even on the best of days, life is complicated. On bad days, everything seems to happen at once. Nothing goes right. Advice comes from friends, parents, teachers, books, television—and it's all different! It's hard to decide what's happening, let alone what to do about it.

Stories help us control our lives. We can snip off small bits and examine them for as long as we like. We can try

as many different ways of dealing with problems as we can think of. Our characters can make our mistakes for us and discover solutions to our difficulties as well as theirs.

• We write to stretch our boundaries.

Writers get to live many lives many times over, their own and those of their characters. A favorite street, smell, sound, day, or friend can turn up in story after story. And characters can venture as far as imagination will take them, carrying the writer right along.

- We write to earn money.

Writing one story or book won't make you rich or famous. Most professional writers are neither, and have jobs other than writing to help pay the bills. But publishers DO pay for well-written stories. And it is a treat to be paid to do something you already love doing!

- We write to share.

Almost all writers want their work to be read. They want to make readers aware of ideas and feelings and events that are important to them. "Look at this bit of life!" they say. "Isn't it wonderful? I don't want you to miss it!" Or "Look at *this* part. It's horrible, and you ought to help change it." Writers work alone, but their goal is to communicate.

- We write because it's fun.

Language is fun to play with. It's one of nature's most thoughtful gifts—an unbreakable toy with a lifetime guarantee. As babies we babble, happy just to hear our own silly sounds. As we grow, we talk and sing and tell jokes and play word games. And we make up stories just to see what happens. Just for the fun of it.

The stories each of us has to tell are unique, like our fingerprints. No two are ever exactly alike. You can't tell my stories; I can't tell yours.

Whether they are happy or sad, gentle or zany, stories are fun to write and fun to read. Even wild stories. But wild words aren't fun. They go out of control and mess up what you're trying to say. With practice, you can tame them and teach them to tell the special stories that only you can write.

I hope you will, because the rest of us are eager to

read what you have to say. Your ability to tell stories is nature's gift to you. The stories you choose to tell are your gift to the world—a gift you can enjoy yourself while giving it away. Be generous!

10

More Books for Young Writers

There are many books available to help you as you continue writing. Most of those on the following list can be found at your local library or bookstore. Bookstores can also special order those they don't have on hand, and libraries may be able to borrow them for you from other libraries. Ask you librarian about a process called "interlibrary loan."

Several books on this list are marked "out of print." You won't find them in stores anymore, but your library may still have copies or be able to locate them for you.

1. Stories

Cheyney, Arnold. *Let's Write Short Stories.* Seamon, 1973. Out of print. Grades four and up. An easy-to-understand book highlighting the basic techniques of story writing.

Dubrovin, Vivian. *Write Your Own Story.* Watts, 1984. Grades four and up. A practical guide to story-writing technique from "Where do I begin?" to "What do you mean, edit?"

Plagemann, Bentz. *How to Write a Story*. Lothrop, 1971. Out of print. Grades five and up. Nine detailed chapters on character, plot, description, conversation, and other "storytellers' tools."

2. Poetry

Cosman, Anna. *How to Read and Write Poetry*. Watts, 1979. Grades five and up. What is poetry? What makes a good poem? This book will help you get the most out of the poems you read and write.

Hughes, Ted. *Poetry Is*. Doubleday, 1970. Out of print. Grades five and up. A poet tells how the ordinary details of life—weather, family, animals—help create poetry.

3. Plays

Judy, Susan and Stephen. *Putting on a Play, a Guide to Writing and Producing Neighborhood Drama*. Scribner, 1982. Grades 5 and up. Everything needed to put on your own show, be it a reading of favorite poems or stories or a full-length original drama.

Korty, Carol. *Writing Your Own Plays: Creating, Adapting, Improvising*. Scribner, 1986. Grades six and up. A serious, thorough look at many kinds of playwriting, from adapting your favorite fairy tales to creating original work.

McCaslin, Nellie. *Act Now! Plays and Ways to Make Them*. S. G. Phillips, 1975. Grades four and up. Easy-to-follow advice on acting, writing, and producing your own plays, skits, and stories.

4. All kinds of writing

Asher, Sandy. *Where Do You Get Your Ideas?* Walker and Co., 1987. Grades four and up. Advice from well-known writers on gathering ideas, and tips on writing stories, plays, poetry, journals, etc.

Benjamin, Carol Lea. *Writing for Kids.* Crowell (hardcover), Harper/Trophy (paperback), 1985. Grades three and up. Fun to read, but also filled with good advice on many aspects of writing, from keeping a notebook to creating a small book of your own.

Cassedy, Sylvia. *In Your Own Words, a Beginner's Guide to Writing.* Doubleday, 1979. Grades six and up. What's special about your world, and what's special about you? This book will help you find out and write about it, too.

Tchudi, Susan and Stephen. *The Young Writer's Handbook.* Scribner, 1984. Grades seven and up. Many forms of writing are discussed—letters, fiction, plays, articles, school assignments—along with information on getting your work published.

Yates, Elizabeth. *Someday You'll Write.* Dutton, 1962. Out of print. Grades four and up. A Newbery Award winner (for *Amos Fortune, Free Man*) answers her young friend's many questions about how books are written and what it takes to be a writer.

5. Others

Aliki. *How a Book is Made.* Crowell, 1986. Grades two and up. Amusing illustrations and a simple text follow a book through its various steps toward publication.

Greenfeld, Howard. *Books: From Writer to Reader.* Crown, 1976. Grades five and up. A fascinating and detailed look at every stage in the process of publishing books.

Hanson, Mary Lewis. *Your Career as a Writer.* Arco,

1979. Grades five and up. Your writing skills can lead to an exciting career in journalism, advertising, radio, television, and more.

Henderson, Kathy. *Market Guide for Young Writers.* Shoe Tree Press, annual editions. A guide to magazines, book publishers, and contests looking for young writers, with excellent advice on preparing and marketing your work.

Melton, David. *Written and Illustrated by.* . . . Landmark Editions, 1985. This one's for teachers, so that they can help students create books. But its many wonderful examples and illustrations from the work of young authors will make you want to get out your pencils, pens, crayons, and paint box and get going!

Purdy, Susan. *Books for You to Make.* Lippincott, 1973. Grades five and up. Easily understood instructions for making your own books by hand.

Index

Marley, 54, 61
"Me and Mr. Nobody" (Melissa
  Harmon)
  comments about the poem, 33
  text of the poem, 22
Melton, David, book by, 106
Metaphors, 87–88
"Monarch Butterfly" (Rhonda A.
  Lee)
  comments about the poem, 77–78
  text of the poem, 77
Montgomery, Beth A., story by,
  39–41, 43, 44
Moore, Kate, story by 16–17
"My Party" (Serina Desch), 12–13

Obstacles, for characters, 95
  importance of, 37–38
  kinds of, 42–43
  the worst, 43–44
Out of place words, 84–85

People soup, as a way to create
  characters, 31–32
Pinocchio, 32
Plagemann, Bentz, book by, 104
Plot(s)
  guidelines for evaluating, 95–96
  how characters make a, 34–62
  Type A, 38–44, 95
  Type B, 52–62, 95
Poetry Is (Ted Hughes), 104
Purdy, Susan, book by, 106
*Putting on a Play, a Guide to
  Writing and Producing Neigh-
  borhood Drama* (Susan and
  Stephen Judy), 104

Reading of stories. *See* Sharing of
  stories
Reasons for writing, 98–102
Rereading, 90
Rewriting (fine tuning)
  descriptions of, 76–77, 88
  editors, the role of, 90–93, 94
  examples of, 77–88

guidelines for evaluating, 96–97
lazy words, 79–83
out of place words, 84–85
show-off words, 85–87
similes and metaphors, 87–88

Scrooge, Ebenezer, 53–54, 59, 62
Sears, Andy, poem by, 22, 33
Sensory images, as a way to show;
  don't tell, 65–68, 72–75
Sharing of stories, 90
  characters, guidelines for evalu-
    ating, 95
  ideas, guidelines for evaluating,
    94–95
  plot, guidelines for evaluating,
    95–96
  rewriting, guidelines for evaluat-
    ing, 96–97
  rules for, 93–94, 97
  show; don't tell, guidelines for
    evaluating, 96
Show; don't tell
  action as a way to, 64, 68–70, 74–
    75
  description of, 63–67
  dialogue as a way to, 65, 70–72,
    74–75
  examples of, 64–66, 70–71
  guidelines for evaluating, 96
  sensory images as a way to, 65–
    68, 72–75
Show-off words, 85–87
Similes, 87–88
Smith, Bryan, story by, 23–25, 33
Smith, Tammison, story by, 45–52,
  54, 59, 61, 62
Someday You'll Write (Elizabeth
  Yates), 105
"Spiders" (Patrick Colvand)
  comments about the poem, 82
  text of the poem, 81
Stewart, Ochiro, poem by, 21, 26

Tchudi, Susan and Stephen, book
  by, 105

109

110